WHY WAIT?

YOUR TIME IS NOW!

Reagan B. Nevels

Manufactured in the United States of America

ISBN 978-1-7325216-0-5

Cover Design: Adam M. Givens
Interior Design: Charles S. Kunene
Cover Image: Diane Y. Zarlingo
Copy Editing: Ariane Lewis

Published by
Premier Publishing, LLC
1101 Pennsylvania Avenue NW, Suite 300
Washington, DC 20004
www.premierpublishing.com

For bulk purchases and special sales, email:
specialmarkets@premierpublishing.com

Dedication

I would like to dedicate this book to my parents, especially my mom. My parents pour so much into me. They both congratulate and critique me so that I will always be my very best and never anything less. I promise to do my best to positively impact the world.

Thank you, Mom. Thank you, Dad.

Love,
Reagan

Table of Contents

Introduction

Why do we put things off? Why do we avoid them and put our dreams and goals on the back burner? Is it because we don't believe in ourselves? Are we afraid of the possible outcomes? Is doubt the cause for the delay? Or not having enough support? I'm sure you'd agree that everyone has a different reason or excuse behind procrastination. We already know life presents all sorts of challenges, but when we focus on finding solutions, we can succeed. **Often, the secret is buried within us and waiting to be discovered.**

When I first made the switch from traditional school to homeschooling, I assumed the transition would be easy. However, instead of doing well in my classes, I found myself procrastinating. Homeschooling required more self-discipline than I was prepared for at the time. I began to skip school and put off assignments until the last minute. I convinced myself I could complete my work in a couple of days rather than spacing out my assignments over time. Before long, I began falling behind.

It didn't take long for me to realize procrastination would not lead to much productivity in the end. I wanted to succeed so I thought about what I needed to do. I decided to write a plan that broke up my assignments so I could do my schoolwork little by little. I spoke positively and I believed in myself. Now, I am doing just as well with my homeschooling as I was back in traditional school. So why did I procrastinate in the first place?

It's easy to use an excuse as a way of escape but that keeps us from working toward our goals. **The problem occurs when we become comfortable living with excuses. Why? We begin to make excuses for anything we want to escape rather than confront.** However, this kind of thinking doesn't give us permission to ignore what we've been called to do. This book is a tool to help you overcome fear and move past challenges to start taking proactive steps toward your dreams right now. My formula of think, write, believe, and achieve will take you step-by-step from the onset of your dream to its fruition. By the time we're done, procrastination will be a thing of the past.

Sometimes we do the craziest things because we are afraid of following through and being successful. Just as people have a fear of failure, they may also have a fear of success. You may ask, "**Why in the world would people have a fear of success?**" There could be many reasons; one might be, they are afraid of the exposure. They could be afraid of the judgment they would face. They could have every tool in the world to help them achieve their goals, but they are simply fearful of the reaction of others. The funny thing is that in most instances, we're focusing on the wrong part of the equation. The real concern is not that we are afraid, but how we address it.

The truth is we have allowed fear to downgrade our abilities. Inside we may feel we are merely mediocre, but we're not. We have extraordinary gifts and extraordinary talents, but we don't want to show them off to the world. So instead, we make statements like, "**Maybe I'm just not ready,**" "**Maybe I'm too old,**" "**Maybe I'm too young,**" or "**No one is going to believe in me.**" Some people put all of these poor ideas and thoughts in their minds and unfortunately begin to believe the untruths of these statements. I've discovered that this is true for both the young and mature in age.

While I hope my message transcends gender and age, I live to encourage young people like myself. It is important that kids are confident in knowing we don't have to wait to reach a certain age in order to accomplish our dreams and goals. I believe this. And I want to show you how you can believe and achieve this, too. Truthfully, my friend, your reflection in the mirror is proof you are much more than what you think. In fact, you are greater than the best image of success your mind can imagine. Pause to visualize yourself being great; now, multiply that by ten. That's where you are destined to be. It's time for you to access the benefits that await you. There's so much you can use to your advantage, but it's up to you to unleash it.

Now, let's spend a moment thinking about the goals you want to accomplish. Don't panic, because whatever your goals are, there is a path to accomplish them. In fact, I'd like to offer my 4-step process to success:

1) Think 2) Write 3) Believe 4) Achieve

WHY WAIT?

YOUR TIME IS NOW!

Reagan B. Nevels

☆

Chapter 1

T.W.B.A.

What is T.W.B.A.? T.W.B.A. is an acronym for a 4-step process I created called: **Think. Write. Believe. Achieve.** This 4-step formula helps me put things into a kind of checklist. When I finish something, I refer back to the formula so I can check it off like people do with grocery lists. For each task I complete, I simply cross it off the list and repeat the process.

Think

Thinking is the process of brainstorming different ideas, dreams, and goals you want to achieve. Once you gather all of your ideas, you have to transform them into positive thoughts. For example, let's say you watch a sad movie about the life of an unlucky dog. Days go by and as hard as you try, you can't stop thinking about it. Instead of putting it out of your mind, pay attention to the thought. Maybe there's a future for you in caring for unwanted or mistreated dogs. Changing a negative experience into a positive vision might just help you discover your true purpose. Your recurring vision may actually be something you have an interest in pursuing. This is helpful because it means we have used our minds for our own greater good. We have made it so we can now think positive! The keyword here is **positive**.

As you work to create positive thoughts, avoid letting ugly excuses form negative ones. You can do this by removing the negative things from your life. Sometimes that can include negative people as well. You may think someone is your best friend, but if that friend is skeptical about what is within your reach, you might want to rethink the relationship.

One way I address negative people in my life is by separating myself from the toxic environment they create and placing myself in a healthy one. Sometimes, that's all you have to do.

Write

The next step is Write. Writing is the process of transferring your ideas and thoughts to paper. This can be hand-written or typed. My favorite method is to type out my thoughts, but it's important you do what's best for you. You can even write first, then type. Whatever you prefer, just write it down.

In my first book, *Vision Collision*, I talk about how helpful it is to create a vision board. Please allow me to make the same recommendation here. Create a vision board! Before we talk about creating one, we have to know what a vision board is, right? A vision board is a collage you create to help you focus your ideas. Don't just put your name on it, make it personal. Use pictures and other visuals that speak to your dreams and goals. So everyone who looks at it will know what you expect of your future. Be sure not to compare your vision board to that of the girl or boy next door. Stay focused on who you want to become and what you desire to accomplish.

Believe

The next step is Believe. You must believe in yourself for this step to work. Besides you, who else in your life believes in you? Do you believe this person will catch you when you fall? Will this person be with you every step of the way, even when times get hard? Better yet, will he or she free you to become great and celebrate your success while also lovingly tell you when you're off track? Who you believe in and who believes in you is crucial to your stability and growth.

As a Christian, I believe in God without apology. I whole-heartedly believe He will continue to provide

the wisdom and guidance I need to make it through any obstacles that may try to overwhelm me. Why do I have such great trust in Him? He never fails to help and guide me. Even though I am not perfect, He has a way of putting me on a perfect path. So, in whom do you place your faith? If not God, does that person believe in you whole-heartedly?

Achieve

The final step is Achieve. Some people might say that achieving is the easiest step when, in reality, it is the hardest. After you think, write, and believe, you have to put everything into motion. You are responsible for getting it done. Yes! You've got it right. Success requires that you take the first step toward where you want to be.

NEWS FLASH: You will have to keep moving in order to get it done! If you want a job during the summer months, it won't come to you if you stay home watching television or listening to music all day.

You must get up and meet the opportunity you want to have. When you do, something positive is sure to happen.

Live in the reality of your faith rather than in the shadows of fear. If you let it, fear will make you slam the door in your own face when opportunity is holding it wide open. Everything fear has to say is false, but everything faith says about your future is the truth. Don't allow excuses to come between you and your future. Waiting is no longer an option. The time is now for you to identify what you want to do and do it. Just as rain finds the ground, success will find you; all you have to do is spot the clouds. Whew! I'm excited just thinking about all the great things you will accomplish.

☆

Chapter 2
Accountability

We began our discussion by addressing and overcoming procrastination. Good stuff, right? We were able to identify a few reasons why people put their dreams on the back burner. We also learned that in order to avoid procrastination, we have to entertain the thought of positive outcomes over negative ones. After reading **Chapter 1**, I hope you will think twice before you put yourself on the path to excuses. Excuses have no right to reside in your future. The truth of the matter is adults and youth alike have to be aware of making excuses. We all should remain intentional about not falling into this kind of thinking.

From what I have observed, adults tend to make taking care of their families their first priority. For that, we are grateful. However, I think it's important for them to remember they are a priority, too. It's important to take care of yourself as you manage daily tasks so you can also pursue your dreams.

This is true for our parents and guardians, and it's also the same for us. Now, young people, you didn't think you would get off the hook that easy, did you? Be careful not to allow something like social media, potential popularity, or sports to become your first priority unless it directly relates to your dreams. If it doesn't, you run the risk of forgetting about your dreams and forfeiting the possibility of accomplishing your goals.

Part of being successful lies in what you do today and how it can help you reach future success. For example, let's say you have the opportunity to take advanced-level classes in high school. Before taking one, you may want to ask yourself some questions. Will this class be beneficial five or ten years from now? Will it provide the foundation for a future career? The answer is yes.

Your education is always an investment in yourself. You're going to be successful because you are doing what you can today to help your future self flourish.

On the other hand, if someone chooses parties, sleeping in, or watching movies over taking an advanced-level class, a future job opportunity may be lost. Hard work and determination are what get us where we want to be. Think about whether what you do today can help you tomorrow. In other words, don't ever let yourself get too comfortable in the present. Instead, accept the challenge of experiencing temporary discomfort to climb the ladder of success.

Don't get me wrong. I'm not saying that you shouldn't enjoy life. What I want to communicate is none of us can afford to remain stuck in a moment of happiness. Yes, we can enjoy school, family, friends, and eat all the ice cream we want. Travel the world if the chance presents itself, but do everything with a commitment to yourself to never become complacent or mediocre. Mediocre means to be just so-so, ordinary. I don't think any of us want to do things or behave in a manner that is merely adequate, right?

Your next question may be, "**How can we avoid becoming mediocre?**" I'm so glad you asked! First, always stay true to yourself and seek out ways to become one-of-a-kind in everything you do. Additionally, keep a positive outlook. When we remain optimistic, we discover we have the grace to achieve a positive outcome in any situation. Negative forces distract the average person, but a person who desires to be different stays focused on the positive. In fact, his or her drive to accomplish specific dreams and goals will eventually drown out voices of negativity. These individuals tend to rise above mediocrity in most situations.

When you attempt to accomplish your dreams, ambitions, and goals, it is almost critical to have two or more accountability partners. These are people who have your best interests in mind. According to Merriam-Webster, accountability is "a willingness to accept responsibility". When we choose people to hold us accountable, their job is to watch and observe what we do. They are the individuals whom we trust to make sure we are on the right track. More importantly, accountability partners often provide us with inspiration and remind us nothing is ever too difficult to achieve. In doing this, they also push us to put in the hard work, effort, and energy required for us to reach positive results. Yes, these are the folks who believe in us when all odds seem stacked the other way.

My mom is my accountability partner. I make sure to share my goals as well as my whiteboard with her. On the whiteboard, I write the steps I am going to take to achieve those goals. She holds me accountable to things I have said

I want to achieve along with the dates by which I want to achieve them. She doesn't force me, but she does give me gentle reminders to keep me on track. And they work!

Remember, I'm here to encourage you. That means I'm also obligated to tell you the truth even when it hurts. Here it comes: **you must invest in yourself.** It's not enough for others to invest in you. You must also take stock in yourself. Never leave the vision for your life in the hands of others. Be ambitious and refuse to let outside factors break you down. The more you invest in your dreams, the greater your feeling of accomplishment will be when they come true.

Part of believing in yourself is trusting in your ability to make your dreams happen. So, you want to score high on a college admissions test? Guess what? You must believe and be confident that you can. Trust that you are intelligent enough to accomplish whatever you prepare for and make your mind up to do it.

Once you get to this place, you will benefit from accountability partners. These people stand beside you to encourage you and make sure you never give up.

Even when a negative thought attempts to creep in—because it will—accountability partners help to ensure you always keep a positive mindset.

Along with identifying your accountability partners, please allow me to be your accountability coach. My dear friend, I trust you will always keep your head held high. When you do this, you position yourself to float above all antagonism. When you feel like quitting, I want you to remind yourself of what you set out to accomplish. Regroup, go after it, and don't stop until you get it. As with any great accountability partner, I'm not going to let a lot of time pass between what you said you want and the steps you need to take to get there. Therefore, please pause to identify the date for your goal. **Time is valuable.** What you do with it will determine the results you obtain.

I'm not going to leave you to figure this out alone. I've created a template to help you remain steadfast. Use this until you develop one of your own. Whatever the case, your template should help identify goals you want to accomplish and the timeframe within which you want to accomplish them. The final step is your plan of action. Are you ready? Let's create an accountability plan:

Accountability Plan Template

______________________________ (Title)

☆ The goal I want to accomplish is

______________________________ (Name the goal)

☆ I want to accomplish this goal by __________ (Time)

on ______________________________ (Date)

☆ To help me with this goal, my two accountability persons are:

1. ______________________________ (Name of person)
2. ______________________________ (Name of person)

Kelly's Accountability Plan

- ☆ The goal I want to accomplish is to become a professional soccer player.
- ☆ I want to accomplish this goal by 8am on September 10 (three years after I graduate from college).
- ☆ My two accountability persons are: Trevor (my closest friend) and Emily (my sister).

Do you remember Kelly from my first book, *Vision Collision?* Kelly's ultimate goal was to become a famous soccer player. Above, Kelly gives us an accountability plan; below are her added notes.

I can depend on Trevor to inspire me and remind me that as long as I am still breathing, I have dreams and goals to accomplish. He'll push me to put in the hard work, time, and effort required. As an accountability partner, he will make sure I stay on track to help me get to the place I want to be.

Emily is going to be the person who will hold me accountable by asking every month (or your preferred time intervals), "What are you doing? Are the choices and decisions you're making working in your favor? Are they producing positive or negative results?" Emily is sure to hold me accountable so I don't spend too much time on activities that do not support my long-term goals.

Now, guys, I'm sure you'd agree that Kelly's template is amazing and self-explanatory. Your accountability partners should be very clear about what's expected of them and what they can expect from you. The more specific your plan, the more likely it is your accountability partners will provide you with what you need. After you create your template, make copies and give them to your accountability partners so they can hold you responsible for your plan of action.

Remember when we talked about making a vision board? It can be another type of accountability plan template. A vision board should highlight your step-by-step process toward success. After you've created one, you should be able to answer the following questions:

- ☆ What is the dream or goal I have the desire to accomplish?
- ☆ When do I want to accomplish it by?
- ☆ Who are my accountability persons?

So, are the two people you have chosen to be your accountability partners going to inspire you to keep running and chasing after your goal? Can you trust them to remind you to work hard so you don't break the promise you made to yourself? If you answered yes, break down the barriers you have built around your heart and allow them to push you that extra mile. I know you can do it! Run, my friend, and finish the race.

☆

Chapter 3

Why Wait?

May I ask a question? Who are you waiting for? Are you hoping and praying someone will magically come and do the work for you? Here I go again, the bearer of bad news (but not really). In order to move past the place you are now, it's crucial you release yourself from the control of people who may try to manipulate your future. It's time to remove yourself from the environments in which people try to pressure you down a certain path. The only person who should be able to dictate when, where, and how you pursue your dreams is you. Get the pen out of their hands and begin to write your own life by putting action items on your calendar. An action item is something you do on a certain day. It is a way of keeping an eye on your long-term goal.

Yes, your destiny has granted you permission to break the chains of your past. No longer will you hold yourself back because of what people have said or done to you. When things come to a standstill, don't give up. Where others have placed periods, replace those periods with commas. This means that something good is coming after what has already occurred. It's important, though, that you don't hold grudges against these people. You must take some ownership when someone else's opinions have control over your decisions because you can't be controlled without your consent. Therefore, you should forgive yourself for everything up until now. Don't stop there; step up and give that controlling entity a huge "**NO!**"

Once you break away from conforming to what other people want, it's vital you don't look back. Some people enjoy being controlled because they find themselves hopeless without certain people in their lives. Controlling individuals create excuses for you and make it easy for you to buy into them. Do you want someone to have that much power over your destiny? If so, this could lead to a life of mediocrity.

How do we fix this? Great question! Instead of allowing multiple forms of social media to control your time, begin to meditate on your goals. Picture a goal in your mind and the potential steps to get there. Meditation will create a safe place for you to receive inspiration, envision your goals, and set a plan of action. Don't limit yourself. Stretch your imagination and think about doing something you've never done before. You're probably feeling like that's easier said than done, right? If so, remind yourself of your worth, your capabilities, and that you're not in this alone.

Hey, it might require you to create ten vision boards before you see your dreams come to pass. I don't know about you, but I'd rather have lots of goals to channel my energy toward rather than dismiss my ideas as a result of disappointment from one poor experience. If one of the ten goals comes to pass, your hard work has been well worth it.

With a positive mindset, begin to gather all the notes that highlight your goals. You can even include goals you had in the past but don't feel a strong desire to accomplish now. It's okay because this allows you to examine where you are in the present so that you can get to where you want to be. It would be a shame for you to keep playing soccer when you've developed a love for basketball. You certainly don't want to keep working toward outdated goals.

You know the next step. Write your dreams and goals as they relate to where you are now. You may be thinking, "Hold on one second. We just did that." You are absolutely right. I forgot to tell you that this process is ongoing. You see, in order to prevent us from waiting on everybody else to make something happen, we have to continually evaluate where we are so we can remain on track toward where we are going. Yes, we wrote down some things before, but we have to keep writing them so we see our dreams come a little closer every day. **It might be helpful to start a journal so you have a central place in which you can keep an account of your goals.**

You have to believe in your cause and the reason behind why your dreams must come to pass. Most of the time, what you've been called to do is bigger than you. In other words, as you receive the benefits of your work, others will be transformed by what you do. For this reason, it's important to have faith that says,

"I can, I will, and I won't wait."

Come on! Declare it and say that with me:

"I can! I will! And I won't wait!"

Say it again.

"I CAN! I WILL! And I won't wait!"

AWESOME!

Now, wholeheartedly believe it and make it happen.

Achievement only happens when we decide not to wait on others to believe in us. We must believe in ourselves. Instead of waiting for someone to give us a handout, we become the hand that lifts other people up. Kick procrastination out of your life to make room for each opportunity. Contrary to the popular saying, the sky is not the limit. There is a place for us beyond what we can see in the present moment. However, we will never discover this hidden truth if we don't dust ourselves off and go for it!

☆

Chapter 4

Prioritizing Your Life

I'm sure prioritizing is a hot topic in every age group. Why? People of all ages want to know how to stay focused on their main goal and not allow minor distractions to detour them. Well, while I hope my advice is a benefit to all, I can only speak with certainty to my fellow youth.

The first thing you should know is you must have a strong and secure foundation. If you don't, whatever you build is sure to crumble when a storm hits. A good foundation allows you to build solid and durable outcomes. A couple of years ago, my parents had an addition put on the back of our house. The first thing they started with was the foundation. It took the contractors quite some time to dig, lay the brick, seal the brick, and make sure everything was sturdy before they built on top of it. I remember them telling my mom that if they did not build the foundation correctly, over time the house could shift and create all kinds of chaos. The same is true for your goals. Your foundation is the ground on which you stand.

Now, there are approximately nine billion people on Earth. Why is this relevant? It's relevant because there are at least nine billion varying priorities at any given time. What a competition! Considering this, you have to be careful not to allow someone else to impose his or her priority upon your plan of action. Just as you choose who to allow in your home, you should be careful with whom you share your dreams and goals. If what they are trying to do doesn't agree, it could cause you to become discouraged. By all means, be bold enough to dismiss anyone or anything that acts as a deterrent to your progress.

The best approach that I've discovered for prioritizing is to create a things-to-do list. You've got it. This involves the second step of the 4-step process, **WRITE!**

A things-to-do list helps to capture everything you want to get done for the day, week, month, or year. Once you've listed your duties or goals, determine what needs to be accomplished first. This helps you to decide which action item to make your top priority.

The purpose of prioritizing is to give you a full view of what needs to be done. Then, you can take a closer look to identify what is in high or urgent demand. **It's as easy as A, B, C, 1, 2, 3.**

A – ALWAYS take time to write out everything you need to do and put each task in ranking order.

B – BE open and honest about what you can accomplish in a given day. Don't overwhelm yourself. Remember, what you don't get done today will become a priority for tomorrow.

C - CONTROL your schedule and don't allow others to trespass on your time.

At the end of the day, ask yourself these three questions:

1

Did my activity agree with my things-to-do list?

2

Was I honest about what I could do today?
(If not, decrease your workload the following day.)

3

Did I allow others to distract or rob me of my time?
(If so, create a plan to prevent this from happening in the future.)

Listen, the prioritizing method takes lots of practice. Some people have this down, but many of us have to deliberately prioritize to stay on course. Don't feel bad.

I prioritize for the next day every night. Then, when I wake up, I govern my activity accordingly. What helps me throughout the course of my day is self-affirmation.

Sometimes, we must remind ourselves who we really are:

I am Adaptable. I am Capable. I am Affectionate. I am Ambitious. I am Strong. I am Compassionate. I am Considerate. I am Courageous. I am Courteous. I am Diligent. I am Empathetic. I am Exuberant. I am Generous. I am Gregarious. I am Impartial. I am Inventive. I am Passionate. I am Persistent. I am Philosophical. I am Practical. I am Rational. I am Reliable. I am Resourceful. I am Sensible. I am Sincere. I am Sympathetic. I am Unassuming. I am Brave. I am Brilliant. I am Intelligent. I am Broad-Minded. I am Calm. I am Careful. I am Charming. I am Conscientious. I am Convivial. I am Creative. I am Decisive. I am Diligent. I am Diplomatic.

I am Discreet. I am Dynamic. I am Easy-Going. I am Emotional. I am Energetic. I am Enthusiastic. I am Fair-Minded. I am Faithful. I am Fearless. I am Friendly. I am Funny. I am Gentle. I am Good. I am Hardworking. I am Helpful. I am Humorous. I am Imaginative. I am Intuitive. I am Kind. I am Loving. I am Modest. I am Neat. I am Optimistic. I am Patient. I am Pioneering. I am Polite. I am Powerful. I am Proactive. I am Observant. I am Quiet. I am Spiritual. I am Self-Respecting. I am Sociable. I am Straightforward. I am Thoughtful. I am Understanding. I am Versatile. I am Warm-Hearted. I am Willing. I am Productive. I am Quick. I am Knowledgeable. I am Logical. I am Outgoing. I am Active. I am Precise. I am Cheerful. I am Exciting. I am Professional. I am Balanced. I am a Leader. I am an Initiator. I am Particular. I am One-of-a-Kind. I am Positive. I am Incredible. I am Forgiving. I am an Achiever. I am Original. I am Consistent. I am a Team Player. I am Cooperative. I am Honest.

I am Direct. I am Motivated. I am Industrious. I am Mindful. I am Responsible. I am Traditional. I am Unique. I am Assertive. I am Mature. I am Objective. I am Studious. I am Trustworthy. I am Attentive. I am Committed. I am Realistic. I am Respectful. I am Confident. I am Thorough. I am Accomplished. I am Articulate. I am Artistic. I am Disciplined. I am Tolerant. I am Unselfish. I am Supportive. I am Talented. I am Collaborative. I am Accountable. I am Hopeful. I am a Force of Nature.

Decreeing and declaring these affirmations will create a certain atmosphere. They will help you form the mindset in which you desire to live. If you want to be in a positive environment, you will because you have spoken it. Just as it reads in Proverbs 18:21, "Death and life are in the power of the tongue." The things we say can be the difference between success and failure.

☆

Chapter 5

Mediocrity? No way!

I know we've talked about mediocrity before, but it's so important to me that you understand just how unique you are. There is nothing ordinary or average about you. In fact, the things you accomplish will be successes other people have never reached before. You may be thinking, "**What do you mean, Reagan?**" It's like baking chicken. Chefs have several different recipes although they are after identical results: baked chicken. A mediocre chef may throw a plain chicken in the oven and simply set the timer. A chef who refuses mediocrity, however, will add seasonings and take special care in its preparation. When it's all over, the outcome is baked chicken, but when you refuse mediocrity in your preparation, the dish is a special meal.

This thinking can also be applied to how we live. You may become a doctor, one of thousands of other physicians, but you will have different interactions with the patients in your care than other doctors. For this reason, it's important not to compare your journey with any other person's journey. **We all have a unique road to travel to arrive at our destination. The challenge you face is to perform in such a way that you become your most extraordinary self.**

When you put forth great effort combined with excellence, you will always shine. The radiance that surrounds you will create new opportunities because people will pick you out of a crowd. It's the difference between a dull diamond and one that shimmers. After a diamond has been worn for a while, it collects particles. This causes the diamond to lose the shine it had from when it was first purchased. Now, it's not as noticeable because it has become average.

However, when the jeweler properly cleans the diamond, it looks brand spanking new! What happens then? People notice that ring even in a room full of other jewelry.

You see, we must pause to dust ourselves off. **Dust away the failure, discouragement, and disappointment.** When we do, we prove there is nothing mediocre about us! We do things in an extraordinary way because that is what we are: **EXTRAORDINARY**.

Declare this with me: ***I am NOT ordinary. I am NOT mediocre. I am NOT normal. I am NOT common. I am NOT average. I am NOT moderate. I am NOT merely adequate. I am EXTRAORDINARY.***

Now, don't get the wrong idea. Superiority is not our goal. We strive for equality just as Dr. Martin Luther King, Jr. fought for. **Yes, we are all equal, but we also have individual gifts and talents to put into motion** that could benefit mankind. We all have the same price to pay in order to fulfill our purpose in life, and that's the cost of hard work! The great news is the varied results are priceless.

Here's an even better report: our uniqueness produces different kinds of extraordinary outcomes. For this reason, we don't have to envy anyone else or wait for good things to be hand-delivered. We can celebrate other people's accomplishments and appreciate when others celebrate ours. Our dreams are waiting on us to rise up and collide with them so they will become our realities.

Just as you created your vision board, you have to create a path that will get you to your destination. Remember when I told you just how unique and extraordinary you are? What this means is that your GPS will always provide you with a slightly different route than that of others. You can't just follow them because you'll find yourself on a path that leads to their destinations.

You might be headed in a similar direction, but you have to be aware and alert enough to know when you should change direction in order to get where you desire to be.

This should be fun. Grab your pen and paper. It's time to create your map, one that is sure to get you where you want to be. Whatever road you take, keep in mind procrastination and mediocrity are not allowed on the journey. The first road you travel down should be called:

"Why Wait? Your Time Is Now!"

Imagine a neighborhood on your map that showcases everything you have an interest in or a desire to create. On one of the streets, there will be clues pointing you in the direction of your dreams. You won't know how long it will take to get across the land of hard work, but one thing's for sure—if you stick to it, you will get there in due time.

As you set out on your journey, be sure to keep a pen and paper close because small details will reveal themselves along the way. You'll find yourself revisiting the list of everything you want to do. Now, you have to commit to doing the research required to gain more insight. For example, if you really love to cook, prepare, and serve meals, maybe you should look into becoming a chef. Perhaps you'd be the perfect candidate to open a high-end restaurant or a fast-food place. Think about what you want to serve. Who would be your competition? Are you leaning more toward fast food or an upscale establishment? What types of customers do you want to attract? Will your restaurant be located in the city or the suburbs? Is it your goal to establish a chain restaurant offered everywhere in the country or just in your immediate city or state? It may be helpful to obtain a mentor in a field related to your goal. Sometimes following your dream means knowing how to ask for help from the appropriate people.

These are just some of the questions we have to think about. **Questions help us move forward.** You will have to apply relentless commitment to yourself and your goals, whether it's starting a business, writing a book, or something else entirely. You have to become the person you want to be. You have to be a person who refuses to give up. Your dreams and goals will eventually pay attention to your hard work and energy. After all, you've given them no other choice. The great news is there is always a positive return on hard work.

Are you ready to commit? Are you ready to give this your all? Don't let your age be a setback, especially young people. Being a child or teenager doesn't mean you can't reach lucrative results. Some may think of your age as an obstacle, but you have to view it as an opportunity. The reality is you will be able to reach some people whom adults will not. Allow your age to work to your advantage. In my experience with public speaking, my age has had a strong impact on the way audiences perceive me. When I speak with older audiences, our interactions have always been positive; however, I have found that younger audiences can be just a bit more challenging. There have been times when they had trouble receiving my message. It was difficult to get much of a response from them. At first, it was discouraging, but I found a way to push past this feeling.

As I said before, everything is about mindset. So if you stop at every single discouraging post you scroll onto, you are never going to accomplish your dreams and goals. You have to focus your mindset on the positive rather than the negative. Once I did that, people began to take note of my message and suddenly my age was no longer a factor. This kind of progress happens when we force doubt and low self-esteem out of our lives.

Youthfulness is not a weakness. So what if some adults may not value your thoughts and opinions because you don't drive a car or pay bills yet.

You are still one of the strongest human beings alive. You simply have to believe in all the good things your future has in store for you.

One of my favorite scriptures in the Bible is Acts 2:17 because it declares that young people "have visions" and older people "dream dreams". You were made to envision great things for the future, and the older generation provides wisdom to help you get there. This is why you can't afford to turn a deaf ear to your parents, guardians, or adults in the village of people who love you.

Strength is a benefit of youth, but sound wisdom and advice from adults work to our advantage as a result of their having more life experience.

Don't wait for someone to tell you it's your time or opportunity. Go ahead and start accomplishing your dreams and goals right now as a young person. If you can see it, you can become it. Here's another way to look at it: this is really the best time to go after what you want because you don't have to pay bills, buy groceries, or take care of a family. Therefore, you have fewer distractions and absolutely no excuse!

Don't allow anything to hold you back.

Identify where you want to go and what you want to do. The only person who can stand between your dream and you is you. So get out of the way and fly high.

Give yourself permission
to become
the best
YOU!

After all, nobody
can become
the best you
except
YOU!

☆

Chapter 6

You Can Do It

It's truly my goal that you not only know what to do in order to accomplish your goals, but that you have confidence in your ability to do it. As a matter of fact, let's pause right now.

Say it aloud: "**I CAN DO IT!**"

Keep saying this until you believe it. This is what I did. I repeatedly told myself I could write my first book even though it wasn't a popular thing for a twelve-year-old to do. I had to look myself in the mirror and vocalize this even when there were some adults saying things that didn't agree with my faith.

I heard comments like, "Oh, she's too young," or "She should wait to attempt to be a motivational speaker."

Can you imagine what my life would've been like at the age of thirteen if I had let these statements drown out my confidence when I first set my goal? I can tell you that it would be totally opposite of what I'm experiencing right now. When they said I was too young, I had to be confident that what I had to share would be a blessing to another young person. When they told me to wait, I had to keep reminding myself to push forward. This is what you have to do. Keep pushing with assurance that what you have to offer is valuable.

Be careful not to allow others to define who you are and what you're supposed to be in life. Some people may even try to force an image onto you, but this is who they want you to be. You don't have to dress or talk like anybody else. Tap into the uniqueness of your own fashion and make it a trend. Study and practice excellent speech and embrace your personality. I've learned that if you stay true to yourself and listen to sound wisdom, others will admire you and want to adopt your successful methods.

When this happens, don't be shady. You know, sometimes as young people, we don't want to share. However, once you are blessed with the confidence to fulfill your dreams, help someone else boost his or her courage. Retired professional athletes are a perfect example of being willing to share information. They no longer play the game, but many of them continue their legacies by becoming coaches, mentors, and friends to new players. Once you become successful in your desired area, be willing to share what you know. You don't have to be intimidated by the growth of others.

Often, people see the fame and fortune that comes with another person's success. What people don't see is the time and effort those individuals put into their dreams to see them realized. **Instead of focusing on the result, try honing in on the steps required to reach it. When** you do, you'll find there is enough room on the earth for all of us to be great.

Oh! I should warn you that you are sure to encounter moments of failure. In other words, you are going to make mistakes. This is okay, and you will be okay if you just keep trying. Sometimes, to figure out how to make something work you must discover all the ways it doesn't work. It's been said that two young Detroit scientists failed over four hundred times before they eventually came up with a winner that millions of people use as a cleaning product—Formula 409. Can you believe they failed at their target goal that many times? Whew! That's a lot. I believe the only thing that kept them going was their confidence that something great would eventually come out of their efforts. I believe the same is true for all of us.

I'm fortunate to travel and speak to diverse audiences, but what many don't know is that I have put a lot of time and effort into becoming the most polished speaker I can be. Truth be told, I'm still working on my delivery. In the beginning, I encountered several moments in which I didn't say a word correctly or missed part of my presentation. When this happened, I didn't let my nerves get the best of me. I kept going. I didn't quit. Instead, I continued to work on getting better.

Thankfully, I have a circle of people supporting me. In addition to my accountability partners, my parents always give me positive feedback while still pushing me beyond my last experience. They don't allow me to flounder in moments of failure, whether big or small.

Remember when we discussed accountability partners? Well, this is another one of their tasks. Make sure you have people in your life that won't beat you down when you make a mistake, but have the skills necessary to build you up. Nobody wants to hear everything they've done wrong. Do your accountability partners share with you what you did right and advise you on how you can become better? My mom and dad always tell me, "You can do it!" You know what? I believe it. When I get discouraged because it seems like nothing is working out, I hear my parents' voices. Then I look myself in the mirror and say, "You can do it!"

Perhaps you're feeling like you won't be successful this time because of how things turned out last time. Not so. You can do it! Maybe your friends have convinced you it's okay to be average. Nope. You can do it! It may seem like everything is working against you, but You can do it! Remember, your destiny is fighting and working alongside you. So why wait? Your time is now! The only requirement to win is your refusal to give up.

I pray that when you experience discouragement or failure, you hear my voice saying, "You can do it."

As a matter of fact,
pause from reading
and look in a
mirror. Point at
yourself and say,
I CAN DO IT!

Conclusion

Well, my friend, we have come to the end of this journey, but it's only the beginning for you. Now, you have to take all you have read and apply it. If you don't, it won't come to pass. Don't let yourself be "that" student who sits in class as the teacher lectures but never takes notes, never executes. I want you to be successful, but you have to want it, too.

Remember, no excuses! Don't allow anything or anyone to hold you back. Be sure to identify your accountability partners. They are going to push you, and by this time next year, you will have transformed into a person doing great things. Procrastination will never be your friend. If you haven't already, break up with procrastination and never open a door for reentry. Yes, slam the door shut to delay and procrastination.

Don't forget to focus on the major things rather than the minor. This will require you to prioritize. Make a list and categorize what needs to be done first, second, third, and so on. As you complete each task, check it off, and pat yourself on the back. Then, keep going! Remember, you can't afford to get comfortable in one happy moment, because there are many more happy moments waiting for you. You aren't mediocre, so you can't settle for average. Always look up and expect the best.

The most important thing to remember is that you can do it. If you think it, you can become it. If you write it, you can make it happen. If you believe it, nothing will stop you from achieving it. I'm so excited about what's next for you.

Why wait? Your time is now!

Before we part, please do me a favor so we can stay connected:

☆ Visit my website: **www.reagannevels.com**

☆ Be sure to subscribe to the mailing list on my website.

Follow me on Instagram **@reagan_nevels**

I really hate to go, but it's time for you to become

GREAT!

Works Cited

☆ "About the Formula 409 Brand." *Formula 409.* The Clorox Company, 2020. https://www.formula409.com/about-us/formula-409/.

☆ Carson, Clayborne and Lewis, David L. "Martin Luther King, Jr." *Britannica.* https://www.britannica.com/biography/Martin-Luther-King-Jr.

☆ *Holy Bible,* The King James Version, 1769.

☆ Nevels, Reagan B. *Address to the Nation's Children. Easter with Reagan Nevels.* April 12, 2020, Canton, OH. Canton: 2020.

☆ *The Merriam Webster Dictionary,* Martinsburg, WV: Quad Graphics, 2016.

Think

Write

Believe

Achieve

WHY WAIT?

YOUR TIME IS NOW!

Reagan B. Nevels

PREMIER
PUBLISHING

CPSIA information can be obtained
at www.ICGtesting.com
Printed in the USA
LVHW070343270121
677475LV00002B/11

* 9 7 8 1 7 3 2 5 2 1 6 0 5 *